FOR YOUR HOME

PAINT AND COLOUR

FOR YOUR HOME

PAINT AND COLOUR

JESSICA ELIN HIRSCHMAN ■ PHOTOGRAPHY BY TIM STREET-PORTER

MEREHURST

Dedication

For my husband, David, who reminds me every day how colourful life can be; and for my parents, who taught me how to make a home.

Acknowledgements

There are many colleagues, architects, and designers who deserve acknowledgement for their contributions to this project. In particular, I wish to express my sincerest appreciation to Maxine Ordesky for her continued guidance and encouragement. Also, thank you to photographer Tim Street-Porter for his experienced observations about colour; to the Rohm and Haas Paint Quality Institute for their prompt assistance; and to the staff at the Michael Friedman Publishing Group, whose collective diligence and talent contributed greatly to this book.

A FRIEDMAN GROUP BOOK

Published 1993 by Merehurst Limited
Ferry House, 51/57 Lacy Road
Putney, London SW15 1PR

By arrangement with Michael Friedman Publishing Group, Inc.

ISBN 1 85391 298 0

A catalogue record for this book is available from the British Library.

FOR YOUR HOME: PAINT AND COLOUR
was prepared and produced by
Michael Friedman Publishing Group, Inc.
15 West 26th Street
New York, New York 10010

Editor: Dana Rosen
Designer: Lynne Yeamans
Art Director: Jeff Batzli
Photography Editor: Christopher C. Bain
Production Director: Karen Matsu Greenberg

Colour separations by Bright Arts (Singapore) Pte. Ltd.
Printed and bound in Hong Kong by Leefung-Asco Printers Ltd.

Table of Contents

Introduction

Great colour schemes have been inspired by a wide variety of sources, from the bold contrasts of a modernist painting to the plays of light typical of a cloudy day. Nature abounds with subtle and vivid palettes, with landscapes providing visual lessons in how different colours can be combined without overpowering individual hues. History is equally rich in stimuli. Books depicting ancient civilizations, art and design movements of the past, or contemporary foreign cultures can all offer inspiration. Museums, magazines, and even jewelry are rich sources of ideas for new colour combinations.

The range of colour available today is remarkable. The colours used in the interior and exterior spaces of a home should, most importantly, reflect the tastes and preferences of the inhabitants. However, there are a few basic guidelines that govern the use of colour in home design. Easily understood and mastered, these principles open up the enormous potential of the world of colour.

Colour Theory Basics

Colour theory is best understood through reference to the colour wheel, which was devised by the seventeenth-century physicist Sir Isaac Newton as a graphic representation of how colours relate to one another visually and scientifically. The ordering of colours on the colour wheel corresponds to the rainbow. Complementary colours lie directly opposite one another on the wheel; analogous colours are adjacent.

The three terms that describe colour are hue, value, and saturation. Hue refers to the position a colour occupies on the colour wheel and is synonymous with its name, such as red, yellow, or blue. Value describes the

Left: Textured surfaces absorb and reflect light differently from flat surfaces, subtly changing the perception and feel of applied colour. Found chairs, carefully sanded and painted to hide wear and tear, appear creamy. The colours seem soft. By contrast, the painted fence derives its visual interest from the rough-hewn surface that suits its natural and earthy hues. **Above:** Different shades of pink reveal how colour can enhance texture. A light shade of pink on the top half of this garden wall outlines the shape and texture of the bricks. A slightly darker shade makes the bottom appear smoother by contrast.

lightness or darkness of a colour and is used interchangeably with tone. Colours of equal value or tone appear as the identical shade of grey in black-and-white photographs. Saturation is the intensity or brightness of a colour, with highly saturated colours usually appearing richer and fuller.

In colour lexicons, hues are discussed as warm or cool. This phraseology relates to the fact that light radiates heat—the more light, the more heat. Red hues are considered the hottest colours. Conversely, blues are described as the coolest colours. Green, made by mixing blue and yellow, can be considered a warm or cool colour, depending upon how it is used. The degree of warmth or coolness of any colour is relative; there are cooler shades of red and warmer blues. It all depends upon the proportion of the hues mixed to achieve that particular shade and what other hues surround that shade.

Choosing and Combining Colour

The human eye can discern as many as ten million colours. Selecting even a few hues for a colour scheme can be confusing, and this task is complicated by the fact that the perception of a colour changes depending upon many factors: the amount and quality of light, the texture of a painted surface, the finish of a paint selected, and even the eye of the observer. The best way to know how a colour will look in a particular room is to tape samples to a wall and leave them there for a few days, checking to see how the colour looks at different times of the day. There are also a few guidelines to keep in mind.

*Lighter colours create a sense of openness and make a room seem larger, whereas darker colours bring the walls closer and make a room seem smaller and cosier. Bright colours can be cheery and uplifting, while deeper tones can have a somber effect upon a room, although today's popular jewel tones often evoke an Old World ambiance rich in spirit.

*Bright colours will generally appear more vivid in strong light. Warm colours can compensate for a lack of light and therefore can be used to cheer up north-facing or cooler rooms, while cool colours can make a warm room feel more temperate and comfortable. Rooms with constantly changing light, such as east- and west-facing spaces, are vulnerable to glare and intermittently intense exposures of light. A good choice for these rooms is a neutral blended from a combination of whites and strong hues; as the light changes, this colour will pick up differ-

ent undertones that will change how the colour is perceived. A wall that looks yellowish in the morning may appear whiter at midday and violet at twilight.

*Cool colours often appear to be receding and thus give a sense of depth to a space. Warm colours, on the other hand, visually bring surfaces closer because they appear to advance. Balancing an equal number of warm and cool colours is a very effective way to make a multi-hued palette appear as one cohesive scheme rather than a mixture of competing elements.

*Interior colour schemes are referred to as related or contrasting. The former includes monochromatic schemes, which consist of varying tones and intensities of one hue, and analogous schemes, which consist of colours adjacent to one another on the colour wheel. Complements and other contrasting colour schemes can provide very dramatic effects, but they can still look harmonious when the hues are of the same saturation or value.

*A good way to add a feeling of cohesiveness to a room or a series of rooms is to paint the walls, ceiling, and trim the same hue. For example, painting interior trim throughout a house the same colour optically minimizes the distance and separation between spaces. Conversely, selecting a different colour for each room will visually separate the spaces.

A lavish use of colour can open up a whole world of new decorating opportunities. The following pages present a wealth of fresh, invigorating ideas for using colour inside and outside the home.

Above: COLOUR AND CREATIVITY COMBINE IN THIS OCEANSIDE HOUSE. IN KEEPING WITH THE HOME'S LAID-BACK SURFER THEME, ARCHITECT BRIAN MURPHY USED ORDINARY STRAW DOORMATS—PAINTED IN WARM TROPICAL COLOURS—TO CREATE AN UNUSUAL AND CASUAL SIDE TABLE.

Palettes, Moods, and Architecture

As a design tool, colour is immensely powerful because of its ability to change the look and feel of a room. Colour can alter a room's architecture in many ways: by enhancing beautiful detail, compensating for a lack of architectural character or masking undesirable features, imposing scale, or delineating space. And the palette—the overall colour scheme—chosen for a room is perhaps the single most important element in establishing its mood.

Colour can be its own geometry, reshaping the boundaries of conventional construction by changing the manner in which the proportions of a room are perceived. Consider the primary colours as an example. Because reds and other warm colours appear to be advancing, they can make walls seem closer and a large room appear more demure. Yellow is perceived as the natural colour of light and generally makes a room feel more spacious. Blues, which fall at the cool end of the colour spectrum, often look as though they are receding, making walls look farther away. Colour can also emphasize particular architectural elements within a room such as handsome trim or create a new geometry composed of the juxtaposition of hues.

Every hue imparts its own personality to the room in which it is used. The palettes featured on the following pages reveal how paint and colour can impact tangibly and intangibly on the character of many different spaces.

Left: It is believed that blue, particularly dark shades, enhances the ability to remember dreams. Bright accent colours and a white duvet cover keep this predominantly blue palette from overwhelming the small bedroom. **Above left:** Yellow is perceived as the natural colour of light. Here, yellow walls reflect the morning sunlight streaming through the windows and brighten the room. **Above right:** Red rooms get noticed. In this dining room, artificial illumination supplied by candles emphasizes the warmth of the deep red walls, making it the perfect setting for entertaining and engaging in lively conversation.

Right: The focal point of this family room is the custom-designed double-sided fireplace. Architect Jeffrey Tohl calls attention to the unusual sculpted shape with a strong, warm yellow, which visually draws the fireplace away from the cooler walls and farther into the room. The yellow also creates a natural frame for flames, which radiate rich reds, oranges, and yellows.

Left: Colour can visually delineate smaller spaces within a large, open room and denote transition between areas. Here, a soft purple architectural element promotes privacy without sacrificing the open feel of the space. **Right:** Architects Craig Hodgetts and Ming Fung highlight a mostly glass bedroom wall with a soft wash of green paint. The treatment adds just enough prominence to the wall's horizontal proportions to keep it from being lost beneath the room's high ceilings.

Left: A YELLOW AND GREEN PALETTE ENHANCES THE SPANISH-INSPIRED KITCHEN OF THIS 1920S CALIFORNIA BUNGALOW OWNED BY HILARY AND MICHAEL ANDERSON. THE GREEN TRIM EMPHASISES THE VARIETY OF STRAIGHT AND ROUND ELEMENTS, HIGHLIGHTING THE ROOM'S INHERENT ARCHITECTURAL CHARACTER.

Left: THE PALETTE AND PATTERNS OF THIS DINING ROOM DESIGNED BY ARTIST ANNIE KELLY ARE A SLIGHT VARIATION ON THOSE OF THE ADJACENT LIVING ROOM, CREATING THE ILLUSION OF A ROOM WITHIN A ROOM. BLUE AND PINK BORDERS IMITATE THE LOOK OF CHAIR RAILS, AN ARCHITECTURAL DETAIL USUALLY SEEN IN MORE TRADITIONAL ROOMS THAT PROTECTS THE WALL FROM BEING SCRAPED BY CHAIR BACKS. **Right:** ALTHOUGH IT MAY APPEAR RANDOM, COLOUR SHOULD NEVER BE ARBITRARILY APPLIED. HERE, COORDINATING HUES HOLD TOGETHER A CRAZY-QUILT COLLECTION OF PATTERN AND COLOUR ACHIEVED THROUGH A SELECTION OF PLASTIC LAMINATES.

Above: TWO HALLWAYS SIMILAR IN THEIR DIMENSIONS ARE FEATURED SIDE BY SIDE TO ILLUSTRATE THE EXTENT TO WHICH COLOUR CAN ALTER THE CHARACTER OF A SPACE. EYE-CATCHING GEOMETRY FILLS THE HALLWAY ON THE LEFT, WHICH WAS PAINTED BY ARTIST GREGORY EVANS. HIS PALETTE OF THREE CONTEMPORARY COLOURS, APPLIED TO PLANES OF VARYING LENGTHS AND WIDTHS, RESHAPES THE AREA'S HORIZONTAL AND VERTICAL SPACE AND DISTINGUISHES ITS PASSAGEWAYS. THE CHOREOGRAPHED PATTERN EXTENDS TO THE FLOOR WHERE THE SAME SHADE OF RED DIVIDES AND EMPHASIZES THE SLENDER WOOD PLANKS. THE HALLWAY ON THE RIGHT, PAINTED WITH COOL BLUES AND GREENS, APPEARS TO RECEDE, CAMOUFLAGING THE WALL'S SLIGHT CURVE. **Right:** ALTHOUGH THEY ARE UNUSUAL SHADES OF YELLOW AND GREEN, THE DUET OF COLOUR ON THE CHECKERBOARD WALL HARMONIZE AND FIT THE WHIMSICAL FEEL OF THIS FAMILY ROOM DESIGNED BY ARCHITECTS HANK KONING AND JULIE EIZENBERG.

BY PARKER AND HART

Above: The palette of this family room, with interior design by Jan Turner Herring and architecture by James Kehr, is achieved through upholstery and accessories. The white walls and ceiling appear seamless, providing a neutral backdrop for the vivid accent colours. **Right:** This dining room's muted walls are the perfect background against which to showcase a collecton of colourful Riviera dinnerware.

White Rock
for sparkling fine beverages
SMILING THRU
PACIFIC MAID
SALT
Ground
PEPPER

Above: DESPITE THE MULTITUDE OF COLOUR AND PATTERN IN THIS FAMILY ROOM, THE OVERALL PALETTE DOES NOT OVERWHELM; THE COMPLEMENTARY GREEN AND RED TRIM BALANCE EACH OTHER AND UNIFY THE ROOM'S COLOUR SCHEME. **Left:** COLOUR AND TEXTURE ENHANCE THE RICH NEUTRAL PALETTE OF THIS CRAFTSMAN-STYLE DINING ROOM BY ARCHITECT LARRY TOTAH. THE THIN BAND OF RUST-BROWN, WHICH IS COMPOSED OF HAMMERED COPPER SHEETS, REFLECTS LIGHT DIFFERENTLY FROM THE MOTTLED WALL TREATMENT LOCATED BENEATH IT (DETAIL ON PAGE 55).

Painted walls can be the perfect canvas for artwork and accessories.

Right: A pearly off-white is a subtle backdrop to vintage furnishings. Small amounts of warm yellows, reds, or browns mixed into white paint will create a warm, soft shade of off-white.

Left: A blue-painted brick wall in the London home of artist Andrew Logan and architect Michael Davis creates a textured surface for equally textured art mirrors. Because the room is open to the sun, the colours appear vibrant.

Right: Green is said to enhance concentration and quiet distractions; it is also thought to be easy to look at and have a calming effect. Bright green works extremely well with bold yellows and golds and is therefore the perfect background colour to highlight this collection of antique frames.

These rooms reflect a very personal, confident use of colour. **Above:** An unusual combination of colours gives this bedroom a striking look. The narrow band of black on the walls and the deep blue-purple bedspread serve as a visual relief, balancing the bolder wall and ceiling colours. **Left:** The palette in Hollywood set designer Jeremy Railton's dining room is dramatic and bold, but because red, blue, and gold are prominent colours in Chinese culture and lore, it is appropriate for the oriental decor. A white ceiling helps to open up the colour scheme and the room.

For Mexican architect Ricardo Legorreta, colour and light are fundamental design tools. This home exhibits his trademark use of colour and illustrates how important the appropriate palette can be in establishing mood and distinguishing architecture. Limestone floors throughout the house function as a neutral visual springboard for the exuberant interior colours. **Left:** Painted lattice located beneath a skylight washes diffused pink light on lemon-yellow walls, creating a constantly changing interplay of light, colour, and shadow. **Above left:** An unusual shade of purple frames and showcases an expanse of glass in an interior hallway. The colour of the glass is enhanced by the lap pool it conceals and the adjacent yellow wall, which makes the purple appear richer and more saturated. **Above right:** This exterior sand-yellow concrete wall has lavender-blue accents that make it appear fluid when viewed from different perspectives.

A riot of colour pervades graphic designer Mick Haggerty's home. **Above:** In keeping with the home's abundant and varied use of colour, each surface and architectural element of this bedroom has been painted a different hue. **Above right:** A bright palette turns an ordinary picnic table into decorative outdoor furniture and links the table to the house's exterior colour scheme. **Right:** Trim painted red, pink, yellow, blue-green, and purple hues mimics the rainbow. **Far right:** The symphony of exhilarating colour plays on in the kitchen. The orange-yellow wall appears to frame the artwork, with the visible brush strokes underscoring the freestyle feel of the picture.

Off the Wall

Nowhere is it written that paint and colour belong exclusively on the walls. Walls do comprise the majority of surface area in a room, but they are by no means the only surface area. Sometimes the most dramatic colour schemes come from the colourful use of other elements; consider ceilings, floors, furnishings, lighting, and accessories as much a blank canvas as a room's four walls.

As architect Brian Murphy, an independent thinker when it comes to melding design and colour, is fond of saying: "You can get a lot of mileage from a dabble of colour applied right." The colour game is as much about ingenuity and individuality as it is about quantity. Painted floors can expand a room's boundaries, add a refreshing decorative touch, or function as an unusual visual centerpiece. By painting surfaces and objects that are generally overlooked, an element of surprise can be brought to a colour scheme. A simple gesture, planned and purposefully executed, can establish the mood of an otherwise nondescript room.

Expanding the ways in which colour can be added opens the door to design creativity. The photographs in this chapter present deliberate and exciting uses of colour meant to inspire.

Left: In architect José de Yturbe's weekend home, potted geraniums cascade down a specially designed, stepped wall in an all-white breakfast room. The flowers' red and green palette, spotlighted by sunlight, creates a dramatic, naturally appealing colour scheme. **Above:** Banana trees provide a spot of tropical colour to a Hawaiian, surfer-style interior filled with unusual design gestures.

Left: In this living room designed by Brian Murphy, classic black-and-white tiles are a small but strong focal point that draws the eye away from the striking purple wall. **Right:** A dream inspired Murphy to suspend eighteen radiant red chandeliers from the ceiling of his white living room. After removing the crystals, he painted the various materials—metal, plastic, copper—a flat white for a consistent base colour. His monochromatic colour scheme unifies the myriad of styles, shapes, and sizes.

FLOORS COMPRISE ABOUT ONE-THIRD OF A ROOM'S VISUAL EFFECT. PAINTED FLOORS CAN EXPAND THE BOUNDARIES OF COLOUR IN THE HOME AND SHAPE A ROOM'S CHARACTER FROM THE GROUND UP. **Above:** ARTIST ANNIE KELLY BEGAN THIS DECORATIVE FLOOR BY INSTALLING PLYWOOD OVER EXISTING LINOLEUM. NEXT, SHE SURROUNDED A MONOCHROMATIC KITCHEN ISLAND WITH A SEA OF WASHED BLUE. THE NEUTRAL BORDER SOFTENS THE TRANSITION INTO THE ADJACENT ROOMS AND FURTHER DISTINGUISHES THE KITCHEN'S UNIQUE PALETTE. **Right:** IN ANOTHER BOLD COLOUR STROKE, BRIAN MURPHY SPLASHED AN ULTRAMARINE ANILINE DYE OVER HIS BLEACHED-WOOD KITCHEN FLOOR. SEALING IT WITH SEVEN LAYERS OF HIGH-GLOSS MARINE VARNISH CREATED THIS MESMERISING LOOK.

Above: Architect Mark Mack visually connects custom-designed wood cabinets to the surrounding room with a soft blue-grey. Interspersing bright yellow brings the mostly monochromatic wall to life, proving that a sprinkle of concentrated colour can add substantial dimension and personality to a room. **Left:** A stairway, often the focal point of a multistory home, is an ideal forum for personal expression. For his own stairs, architect Barton Phelps created a palette symbolic of the wooded hill on which his home stands—deep forest-green solid vinyl flooring on the stairs and grey-green paint on the walls. Industrial sconces, inverted and painted white, symbolise clouds. The dark-coloured stairs draw the eye down and add to the feeling of descent, while the lighter walls give the illusion of rising up.

Right: Exquisite architectural details deserve distinctive finishes. These hand-crafted hardwood balustrades were designed and coloured by Mexican architect Luis Barragán. Painting one side of each piece blue adds distinction to the woodwork and stairway.

Right: In this family room designed by Mark Mack, colour enhances the architecture, adding interest to the stairs, floor, bookcase, walls, and folding shutters.

DIEGO RIVERA
ANDY WARHOL
A RETROSPECTIVE

Left: A bright palette reminiscent of brand-new crayons colours a contemporary handrail in an atrium playroom. This structure introduces a youthful, lighthearted spirit to the otherwise neutral palette and dances colour up to the next level, where similar shades enhance the small, square windows. **Right:** In the same home, high-gloss paint covers basic wall-hung bookshelves, making a bold statement out of an ordinary architectural detail.

Ceilings do not need to be limited to white or off-white. Other hues can create unique optical effects and change the character of a room. **Above:** Painting a ceiling a light colour can make it appear higher, whereas a dark colour will make it seem lower. In this room, painting the ceiling and floor the same colour creates the illusion of suspended space. **Left:** In this room designed by Annie Kelly, the continuation of the ceiling colour onto the top portion of the walls shrinks the vertical dimensions by making the ceiling appear lower and the walls shorter. The thin ocher band visually attaches the bottom of the room to the top.

Many areas of the home are overlooked when colour is considered. Painting the interior of a bookcase or display cabinet can add a controlled amount of colour to large or small rooms. **Left:** These cubbies were custom painted to display the collection of pre-Columbian figures. Blue often denotes royalty, and thus seems a fitting choice for the valuable artwork. The serene uniform background feels appropriate, as many of the figurines are depicted in calm and meditative poses. **Right:** Colour and design meld past and present influences in a remodelled family room. Architects Scott Johnson and Margot Alofsin painted the cubbies of two wood display cases in hues that complement the decorative glass and ceramics that they contain. Presenting the palette in a different pattern within each bookcase adds variety and interest without tipping the room's balanced design. From a distance, the bookcases appear as small beads of colour that help lower the perceived height of the cathedral ceiling.

PASSAGE

ANCIENT ROME

Decorative Techniques

For centuries, artisans and craftsmen have embellished interior surfaces and furnishings with fanciful decorative paint treatments. These eye-catching techniques remain popular today for hiding or enhancing design details, taking a room to another time or place, or simply adding a touch of panache to a staid decor.

Decorative painting techniques fall into two categories. Faux (French for "false") finishes—including faux marbling, faux woodgraining, and trompe l'oeil (meaning "to fool the eye")—mimic a real material or object. Trompe l'oeil is a particularly captivating technique that creates realistic focal points or vistas through a freehand application or the use of stencils. Marbling and woodgraining are ideal for simulating sumptuous surfaces without the expense of costly building materials.

The second category of decorative painting techniques includes treatments that do not simulate but simply adorn. Perhaps the most popular and easily achieved treatments are stencilling and colourwashing, which add flourish and a homemade feel to surfaces and furnishings. Stencilling is considered one of the most versatile painting techniques and is certainly one of the easiest ways to add a decorative border or pattern to a painted surface. Colourwashing walls or furniture—applying a diluted colour to a neutral base coat with rags, sponges, or brushes—gives them a brushy, cloudlike appearance and is particularly popular in country interiors.

These are by no means the only techniques available. As the following photos attest, there is no limit to what can be accomplished with paint, colour, and an artistic eye.

Left: Walls and canvas screens painted with trompe l'oeil by artist Julian Latrobe encircle a classical interior designed by Hutton Wilkinson. The illusionary landscape turns the elegant living room into a Roman temple at sunset. The off-white and golden hues look exceptionally warm when gently lighted at night. **Above, left and right:** Trompe l'oeil book spines conceal shelf-size speakers in the home of the late master lyricist Ira Gershwin. Actual books were copied in detail, down to the publisher and author.

Left: A combination of decorative paint techniques—stencilling, colourwashing, freehand design, and trompe l'oeil—epitomizes the creative power of paint and colour. Doors become whimsical portraits, and walls turn into shimmering frames. **Right:** A technique known as faux marbling, which imitates the luxurious look of marble, carves out a stunning fireplace in colours new to Mother Nature's quarries. The imaginative swirling and rich colours add texture and drama to the fireplace, making it a focal point for decorative accessories and furnishings. Artist Steve Shriver's artful shading of the gold-painted accents on the mantel gives the illusion of dimension.

GARDEN STYLE
PENELOPE HOBHOUSE
Landscaping the American Dream
The POETICS of GARDENS

Below: Trompe l'oeil can be used to transform an architectural element into something special. Here, an ordinary pantry door is disguised as a window to thf outside, displaying farmland and a cow peering curiously inside.

Left: Elsie deWolfe, a pioneer in the interior design field, produced this ornate custom writing desk. The dark green interior cubbies resemble tiny, plush jewel boxes displaying their precious contents. Intricate stencilling embellishes the panels. Placed against a colourwashed wall, the cabinet appears even more fanciful. **Above:** Annie Kelly's studio features a hand-painted wall and a cubist-inspired, hand-painted cabinet. Classic stripes of vivid yellow and white create an outdoor, sunny feeling that plays against the cabinet's blue-grey mural.

Left: A custom hand-painted china hutch cheers up a Mexican veranda with colours and patterns reminiscent of Mexican textiles and pottery.

Right: Simple, unpretentious finishes on wood furnishings complement country and rustic interiors. The deliberate chipping away of paint adds texture and a sense of agelessness to this old cabinet. The brushy blue wash covering the wall is a soft and gentle background for the room's open, airy feeling.

Right: There is no reason why decorative paint techniques should stay behind closed doors. Here, a trompe l'oeil throw rug drapes garden stairs at the Acapulco home of Mexican architect Marco Aldaco. Keeping the risers fairly plain and restricting the hand-painted pattern to the treads makes the imaginary carpet appear more realistic. **Below:** The right colour and paint treatment can help mask a rough surface; a delicate pink wash softens this concrete fireplace.

Right: Architect Larry Totah washed a plaster wall with muratic acid, scraped away the existing paint, and veiled the wall—since dimpled from the acid—with diluted water-base paints. Although the treatment began as an experiment, the result appears well thought-out (overview on page 20). The chair was designed by Jon Bok.

Exteriors

A home's exterior gives the first impression of its contents. The shape, colour, and texture of exterior surfaces and design elements can say as much about a home as its interior architecture and palette. The selection of a colour scheme for the outside of a house should be as deliberate as it is for the interior palette.

Exterior colours can be chosen for their ability to link a home to its surroundings or architectural history. The palette might evoke a regional heritage or be compatible with nearby landscapes. For a house that has been remodelled, exterior paint might be chosen to connect the original structure to or distinguish it from the addition. As they do on the inside, paint and colour on the exterior can change the perception of a home's overall size and proportions, highlight certain aspects of the architecture, or make allusions to a bygone era. And paint and colour used outside of the home can add a sense of design where it's least expected, such as to a fence or roof.

When choosing colour for outdoor surfaces, it is important to consider the impact of daily and seasonally changing light. The sun produces intense light in areas close to the equator; in areas farther away, especially in winter months, it is more muted and grey. The texture of building materials can also alter the perception of colour due to the interplay of light and shadow. Fortunately, many of today's paints are formulated to preserve colour against the elements, so aesthetics can take priority.

The homes and exterior features on the following pages represent a range of palettes and applications, illustrating how colours look on expansive surfaces, how paint influences architecture, and above all, why the choice of exterior colour should be made thoughtfully.

Left: Extending an interior colour to an exterior entrance smooths the transition between indoor and outdoor spaces. Carrying the same colour to the ceiling on either side of the door gives the effect of seamless construction. **Above:** Time and weather impact exterior colours, sometimes with wonderful effects. The faded salmon facade of architect Brian Murphy's home is actually the result of decades of weathering. Cool yellow- and blue-painted window sashes, a refreshing visual break, punctuate the exterior of the house.

EXTERIOR PALETTES CAN BE AS VIVID AND IMAGINATIVE AS INTERIOR ONES. **Above:** ARTIST PETER SHIRES APPLIES HIS EYE FOR COLOUR TO HIS FORMER TRACT HOME IN LOS ANGELES. THE STRONG TROPICAL COLOURS HE HAS CHOSEN REMAIN VIBRANT IN THE BRIGHT CALIFORNIA SUNLIGHT. **Right:** ARCHITECTS CRAIG HODGETTS AND MING FUNG USE A CONTEMPORARY PALETTE TO COMPLEMENT THE STRUCTURE AND DESIGN OF THIS MODERN HILLSIDE HOME.

Left: MANY VICTORIAN HOMES ARE AS MEMORABLE FOR THEIR INTERPLAY OF COLOUR AND ARCHITECTURE AS FOR THEIR DISTINCTIVE SHAPES. THIS HOME IS NO EXCEPTION. TOUCHES OF YELLOW, SHADES OF VIOLET, AND BRIGHT WHITE EMPHASIZE TRIM AND OTHER DECORATIVE DETAILS.

Left: IN AN IRONIC STATEMENT, THE PALETTE CHOSEN FOR THIS FUNKY DESERT HOUSE DESIGNED BY ARCHITECT JOSH SCHWEITZER SYMBOLIZES THE BASIC COLOURS FOUND IN NATURE: THE POWDER-BLUE BUILDING REPRESENTS THE SKY, THE YELLOW CHIMNEY EVOKES THE SUN, THE GREEN CENTER STRUCTURE SUGGESTS GRASS, AND THE SMALL ORANGE BUILDING MIMICS THE COLOUR OF CLAY FOUND IN DESERTS AND DRY ENVIRONMENTS.

Left: Mexican lore holds that certain colours ward off evil spirits, and for this reason they are traditionally used inside the home. This solid-looking backyard wall painted a colour called azul añil functions as an amulet protecting a Mexican home. Contrasting vertical red bands reinforce the garden wall's formidable appearance.

Right: The blue colour of this pigmented plaster wall was carefully mixed to approximate as closely as possible the colour of the pool beyond. The wall separates the entrance court of this home designed by Franklin D. Israel from the private backyard, and like worn blue jeans, fades pleasantly over time.

Below: A colourful roof can set a home apart from or, as shown here, help it meld with the environment. The collection of hues in this patterned, multicoloured tile roof allows the home to blend with the surrounding sand and palm trees.

Above: The pervasive use of a warm shade of green turns an ordinary garden trellis into landscape architecture outside this home designed by Mark Mack. Shading the terrace a matching green unifies the house and garden.

Left and below: THESE TWO HOMES LOOK LIKE NEGATIVES OF ONE ANOTHER. GREEN IS USED AS AN ACCENT COLOUR ON THE HOUSE BELOW, RESEMBLING ICING PIPED ONTO A CAKE AND CALLING ATTENTION TO THE HOME'S DISTINCTIVE LINES AND ANGLES. GREEN IS THE PREDOMINANT COLOUR OF THE HOUSE ON THE LEFT, WITH WHITE EMPHASIZING THE DETAILING OF THE WOODWORK AND ROOF.

Left: GREEN IS A NATURAL CHOICE FOR BLENDING HOMES WITH LUSH FOLIAGE. HERE, THE EYE IS DRAWN NATURALLY FROM THE DARK GREEN OF THE HOUSE TO THE SURROUNDING LANDSCAPE. THE WHITE SURFACES ARE A REFRESHING INTERLUDE FROM THE MANY SHADES OF GREEN.

Above: ARCHITECT FRANKLIN D. ISRAEL DESIGNED A SERIES OF INTERCONNECTED PAVILIONS FOR THE REMODELLING OF THIS HOME, WITH COLOUR SIGNALLING A CHANGE OR VARIATION IN THE ARCHITECTURE. THE PALETTE REPRESENTS THE THREE PRIMARY COLOURS: MUSTARD-YELLOW PLASTER SURFACES, REDWOOD-STAINED CEDAR, AND A BLUE GARDEN WALL. **Right:** A PATIO WITH AN OUTDOOR FIREPLACE EVOKES THE FEELING OF AN OPEN-AIR LIVING ROOM. ARCHITECT JEFFREY TOHL HAD THE PLASTER AND WOOD FEATURES PAINTED THE SAME RICH TERRA COTTA COLOUR, BLURRING THE BOUNDARIES BETWEEN THE DIFFERENT SURFACES AND TEXTURES. THE EARTHY HUE ALSO PROVIDES A NATURAL COMPLEMENT TO THE GREEN GRASS.

Left: Mother nature is the consummate colourist, forever combining colours into breathtaking, captivating palettes. A shimmering sunset in Careyes, Mexico, is filled with hues of pink, blue, yellow, and violet. The pastel colours inspired architect Marco Aldeco to wash a residential rooftop in cool hues of blue and purple. The stark-white edge abruptly divides the vista and cleanses the eye in preparation for the colourful, dynamic horizon beyond.

Appendix: Paint and Colour Facts

Selecting the Right Interior Paint

The finish of a paint affects the look of a painted surface and impacts on its maintenance. The higher the paint's sheen, the more the texture of the painted surface will be accentuated, but the easier it will be to keep clean. Paint manufacturers use different terms to describe paint sheen, but most paints fall into one of four categories: flat, eggshell or satin, semi-gloss, and gloss.

Flat Paints

These nonreflective formulations, which tend to camouflage surface imperfections, are recommended for walls and ceilings. Since it can be challenging to remove stains from flat paints, it's wise to restrict them to low-traffic areas.

Eggshell or Satin Paints

Compared to flat paints, eggshell and satin finishes have a more lustrous appearance and are more stain-resistant. Their sheen is slight, however, making these paints attractive in rooms where a subtle shine is desired. They can be gently wiped clean.

Semi-gloss Paints

Because of their higher sheen, semi-gloss paints are even easier to clean than eggshell or satin paints and are often recommended for areas vulnerable to wear and tear, including kitchens, bathrooms, hallways, and children's playrooms.

Gloss Paints

As the name implies, these paints have the highest sheen. Although the look doesn't suit all interiors and their high reflectivity emphasises surface imperfections, these paints are among the toughest, most durable formulations. Gloss surfaces are excellent for high-traffic areas and trim such as handrails or doorjambs.

What Colour Says and Does

One of the virtues of colour as a design tool is its unique ability to evoke meaningful associations, provoke particular physiological responses, or serve as a symbolic reference. These effects can all determine how colour is used in a decorating scheme. Understanding the meanings of different colours is a precursor to selecting a pleasing palette. It's also just plain fun.

Red

An emphatic colour, red signifies both danger and romance. It is the colour of courage and conviction. Red excites: sustained exposure to red hues is believed to increase the flow of adrenaline in the bloodstream. Restaurateurs believe that red hues stimulate appetite and conversation. Red is compelling, and it can create strong architectural focal points in a room.

Yellow

The most reflective of all colours, yellow is perceived quickly—it has immediacy and urgency. Yellow cheers and lifts the spirits. It is the colour most often associated with the sun, hence it is perceived as the true colour of light. Like red, yellow speeds up metabolism and is often used—in appropriate shades—for kitchens and dining rooms. The Sung Dynasty honoured yellow as the imperial colour, which may explain why it is symbolic of intellectual and spiritual enlightenment.

Green

Green is symbolic of life, fertility, and rebirth. Green hues seem appropriate for interiors largely because they are so abundant in nature, where they act as peacemaker, harmonising a parade of colours. Physiologically, green is said to have a soothing effect on the eyes and mind, filtering out distractions and enhancing concentration. Greens often make good backgrounds or accents in multihued rooms.

Blue

Infinitely popular and multifaceted, blue looks good almost anywhere, and because it's associated with the sky and ocean, it feels natural on expansive surfaces. Blue can evoke feelings of peace and tranquillity and can at other times represent sadness. Blue can be incorporated into a high-tech design scheme as easily as it can appear fresh and unpretentious. Cobalt and Wedgwood blues are particularly popular in decorating schemes. Certain Eastern cultures believe blue to be the colour of immortality. The Egyptians cherished blue, and even today it remains symbolic of royalty.

Violet and Purple

Perennially popular at Easter, purple was once the colour of things ecclesiastical. Roman emperors and nobles of many cultures favoured purple robes as an indication of privilege and power. Some psychologists suggest that purple is the colour of introspection and internalisation. In design, deep shades of purple or violet are generally seen as accent colours, while lighter shades work well on larger surfaces.

Black

Always classic, black is as much of a basic element in home design as it is in the fashion world. While black is technically not a colour because it is devoid of light, it does affect mood and spatial perceptions just as true colours do. Black symbolises death and wickedness but it can also suggest elegance and opulence. Colourists, designers, and painters use black as a catalyst for achieving different shades: the process of shading, adding black to a colour, makes it deeper and darker.

White

While white is the colour of mourning in some cultures, in Western philosophy it is the essence of purity and fresh beginnings. White is composed of the entire spectrum of light, which accounts for its many personalities. Depending upon the shade, white can be stark and sterile or clean and refreshing, and it will generally make a small room feel significantly larger. Because white is the starting point of so many wonderful custom colours, it has been called the decorator's work horse. The process of adding white to a hue is known as tinting.

Neutrals

These palettes are often overlooked and underrated. Neutrals are exceptionally easy to live with, and are ageless, graceful, and rarely offensive. Their subtle, unobtrusive appearance makes them an ideal foil for furnishings, art, or decorative paint treatments. Today's neutrals are often custom blended from many hues, each of which imparts its own cast and colour to a painted surface as light moves across it.

Index